the winds of change

Assia Boukrouh

THE MIZAAN

"The Winds of Change"

Copyright © [2024] Assia Boukrouh - The Mizaan. All rights reserved. No part of this publication may be reproduced, distributed, or transmitted in any form or by any means, including photocopying, recording, or other electronic or mechanical methods, without the prior written permission of the publisher, except in the case of brief quotations embodied in critical reviews and certain other noncommercial uses permitted by copyright law.

Disclaimer: The views expressed in this publication are those of the author and do not necessarily reflect the official policy or position of any other agency, organisation, employer, or company.

Dedication

To my father, who believed in me when I didn't believe in myself and who I miss more than words can express.

To my mother, who is the apple of my eyes and whose arms will forever be my safe place.

To my sister, who I can't imagine my life without and who held me when I was at my lowest.

I love you with all my heart.

Acknowledgments

I have to start by thanking Allah ﷻ for choosing me everyday to be Muslim, for having planted these seeds in my heart and having guided me towards this mission.

Thank you to my family and close friends, who have loved and supported The Mizaan before I had even started it. I know you think I'm a little crazy sometimes and work too much, but you never failed to stand by my side and consider my wins as yours.

And of course, thank *you*, my dear community. I wouldn't be where I am without your messages, your comments and your prayers. I will never forget your kindness, generosity and sincerity. You've done more than you can imagine for me.

Preface

So here we are. The big 30.

I still have to wrap my head around the fact that my twenties are over. I used to always freak out about getting a year older and witnessing time slipping through my fingers. The over achiever and dreamer that I'd always been felt frustrated when it was time for a new birthday, because I never felt content with what I had accomplished. It was never enough. Each one was just another countdown before the deadlines I had set for myself. "I'm 25 and still not finished with my studies", "I'm 26 and still don't have my driving licence", "I'm 27 and still not married", "I'm 28 and still haven't reached my ideal income"... But surprisingly, when I turned 29, this didn't happen.

Facing death for the first time a few months prior had certainly made me realise how nothing matters that much in this life, except Allah ﷻ. All these worries that I'd had my whole life, thinking that my worth was only defined by my achievements, suddenly seemed very small and started to feel lighter. It gave me a new sense of purpose and reignited what has always been my mission with my work: finding balance.

I knew that turning 30 was still a big deal to me though so I wanted to make it count, to do something that wasn't just an act of love to myself but also to my community who's stood by my side.

For the past four years, The Mizaan has been like my online diary, a space where I finally felt safe to be the overthinking, sensitive, introverted girl I had always been. Seeing all these women around the world from different ages and cultures relating to my words made me think they deserved to be more than just pixels on a screen.

I'm not going to lie, this book is not a great piece of literature, and please don't expect it to be an Islamic knowledge resource. However, it is a token of my gratitude to you all and a little gift to myself: I've gathered all the life lessons, reflections, big sister advice, lengthy captions and posts I wrote and that you were all touched by in here. This is for whenever you need to remind yourself that there's a soul out there who knows how you feel, who loves Allah ﷻ just as much as you and craves to improve everyday for His sake, even if it isn't always easy.

Reading my texts again when compiling them, adjusting them and adding a few new ones along the way made me realise how much I've evolved during my twenties, and it made me smile. Knowing that sharing my journey somehow contributed to the growth of another sister has to be one of the greatest honours of my life, and it made me cry (in a good way!).

I hope you'll enjoy reading my humble words as much as I enjoy sharing them with you. Know that I love you for the sake of Allah ﷻ and pray that your life, in this dunya and in the Akhirah, will be filled with joy, tranquility and love.

Assia

Your life might not look like what your younger self hoped for, but your younger self hadn't lived enough to know was best for older you. Indeed, we plan, but Allah ﷻ is The best Planner. So, show yourself some mercy and be grateful for the journey, always.

It is all about balance.

Sometimes I think about the time where Islam was part of my life but not the center of it. I had always thought that being Muslim was just a facet of my identity, that it didn't have to define who I was as a person.

Back then, Islam was my religion, but not my way of life. It was like having a bouquet of dried flowers in my home: it was there, it was beautiful, it brought me joy and comfort, but I was not giving it any maintenance. It was not alive, it didn't grow. I didn't get any credit for it.

I simply lived with it, not *for* it.

For a long time, I unconsciously reassured myself by thinking that having a bouquet of dried flowers was better than plucking a flower and seeing it die. I guess it is, but why would I compare my bouquet to someone who doesn't even care that much about the flower in the first place instead of someone who planted the seed, watered it and saw it bloom?

So, as much as I love dried flowers (there are in fact a great piece of home decor haha!) I just felt like what I truly needed was cultivating my own ones. Of course, I knew that flowers wilt, that the weather isn't always bright. But that's how everything works in this life. Without seasons, you wouldn't witness the rain watering your meadow; you wouldn't appreciate the petals slowly unfolding; you wouldn't experience the joy and relief of seeing your garden finally flourishing after so much effort put into it.

Same goes with your *imaan*: as long as you keep nurturing it, even in dim and cold days, rest assured you'll always see it gracefully blossom into a splendid bouquet of strength, resilience, serenity, and love for your soul to cherish. As Asma bint Abu Bakr (ra) said: *"Verily my happiness is my imaan and my imaan is in my heart, and verily my heart does not belong to anyone but Allah ﷻ."*

1. Gratitude	....	13
2. Acceptance	....	17
3. Kindness	....	24
4. Doubt	....	28
5. Modesty	....	35
6. Womanhood	....	41
7. Resilience	....	47
8. Forgiveness	....	52
9. Introspection	....	58
10. Community	....	63
11. Humility	....	68
12. Discipline	....	74
13. Purpose	....	81
14. Sincerity	....	87
15. Confidence	....	91
16. Justice	....	99
17. Knowledge	....	104
18. Family	....	108
19. Respect	....	111
20. Comparison	....	114
21. Intentions	....	118
22. Mindfulness	....	122
23. Consciousness	....	125
24. Stewardship	....	129
25. Contentment	....	132
26. Grief	....	135
27. Hope	....	140
28. Loneliness	....	143
29. Trust	....	147
30. Love	....	151

This page was left blank intentionally.

Gratitude

Alhamdulillah — The power of this word always amazes me.

One of the things I truly appreciate about the commands of Allah ﷻ is how they not only serve as a way for us to praise Him but also to preserve ourselves from the torments of this dunya.

Counting your blessings daily and thanking Him for them certainly makes you humbler, brings you closer to your deen, strengthens your bond with Him, and therefore, softens your heart.

That isn't the only reason why Allah ﷻ wants you to say Alhamdulillah though: many studies now show the mental and physical benefits of practicing gratitude (e.g., reduced blood pressure, increased sleep quality, improved emotional and psychological well-being...). This means that it not only positively impacts your relationship with Allah ﷻ and others but also with yourself. Each time you say Alhamdulillah, you're giving yourself two gifts: the gift of self-love for His sake and the reward that goes with it.

Isn't it amazing?

Be grateful for everything. Absolutely everything.

Be grateful for the people in your life because if you're not, it is as if you're not grateful to Allah ﷻ.

Be grateful for the smallest things because Allah ﷻ will ask you about them on the Day of Judgment.

Be grateful for your trials because Allah ﷻ tests those He loves the most.

Be grateful for being Muslim because out of billions of souls, Allah ﷻ chose yours to be part of the Ummah of the best man He's created.

Being grateful for everything in your life will completely transform it and take you to a place you never thought existed. Think of it as the Islamic approach to the classic growth mindset or to manifestation: the more grateful you are, the more you'll get in your life. This is His Promise.

The moment you realise that All Praise is due to Allah ﷻ, your mind becomes clearer, and your world truly becomes brighter. Subhan'Allah ﷻ, Alhamdulillah, Allah ﷻu Akbar.

"IF YOU ARE GRATEFUL, I WOULD CERTAINLY GIVE YOU MORE."

(14:17)

"AND HE GAVE YOU FROM ALL YOU ASKED OF HIM. AND IF YOU SHOULD COUNT THE FAVOR OF ALLAH ﷻ, YOU COULD NOT ENUMERATE THEM. INDEED, MANKIND IS [GENERALLY] MOST UNJUST AND UNGRATEFUL."

(14:34)

"AND WHOEVER IS GRATEFUL IS GRATEFUL FOR [THE BENEFIT OF] HIMSELF."

(31:12)

Acceptance

I've always been the kind of person to use 'why' a lot — *why this, why that, why me, why us, why them...* Some find it endearing, others find it annoying but funnily enough, it personally led me to wonder *'Why am I like this'*?

For a long time I thought it was only curiosity, but then I realised it was deeper than that: it was actually my constant need to understand so I can better anticipate and therefore better control the emotions I'm willing to display and the outcome of my decisions.

I know how easy it is to think *"ya Allah ﷻ why?"* or *"this is so unfair I don't deserve this"* when you're going through something difficult, and as much as we say *"Astaghfirullah"*, we still can't find complete peace of heart.

I've been there and it took me the biggest hardship I've ever been through to realise that while asking forgiveness is essential, it doesn't stop there.

Honestly, I would have never thought my dad's cancer would bring me this close to Allah ﷻ. It showed me how your whole life can change in the blink of an eye, how important it is to detach yourself from this dunya, how you should be grateful for every new day you're given and how you shouldn't waste time not pleasing Him.

Obviously there's still a long way to go and some days are rougher than others. Yet, Allah ﷻ would never lie to us and He did say He wouldn't burden a soul beyond that it can bear, right? So don't just apologise: persevere, look for the beauty surrounding you and keep in mind that absolutely everything happens for a reason, even if you cannot comprehend it right now.

We know Islam is a religion of discipline, that requires you to be in control of yourself and it might be the reason why I connect deeply with our deen Alhamdulillah, despite the weaknesses and struggles that come with being Muslim in this dunya. However, in order for this to not turn into frustration, anxiety or anger, we need to learn to accept.

His Qadr encompasses everything and is a continuous reminder that we're only human. May He bless our hearts with inner peace and Sakinah.

You know, I've been working a lot on my struggle to accept not always finding an answer to my questions, especially when it comes to people. I just can't help but thinking *"what is this person actually thinking deep down?"*, *"why are they acting like this?"*, looking for a reason to explain their behaviour when it is incoherent, disrespectful, intolerant or hurtful.

Although it took me time to accept not being able to help everyone, I got there Alhamdulillah, but *this* — not knowing the reason why someone would behave a certain way or wrong me this much — has honestly been pretty challenging. I used to be this stubborn kid who would stick to a math problem until I solved it, even if it meant spending hours on it. But the thing is, you cannot figure out minds like you would with math.

I think the hardest part of this is facing the possibility of people being genuinely careless with a soul that trusted, appreciated or even simply respected them. I mean, this might sound very cheesy, but why would you choose to treat people badly when you can be kind? Why would you be this neglectful about a person's feelings if it wasn't because of the war you're having against yours? There's a way to address people even if you disagree or if you prefer to grow apart, why would you choose to speak despicably? Where has your humanity gone?

It's easier to blame unsolved trauma and a sick heart clearly longing to find peace or to tell yourself this person was simply odious and hold grudges against them, rather than letting it go, right? Well yes, sometimes, you are simply a collateral damage in somebody's battle against themselves and sometimes you're just a test they miserably fail. But the truth is, it doesn't really matter what's the reason behind their actions: we need to accept it without desperately trying to crack their codes or refusing to heal from the disappointment we feel towards them.

At the end of the day, they serve as a proof for us that only Allah ﷻ knows what lies in our hearts. If they're behaving this way, it might be a picture of the state of theirs but also, a sign for you to check on yours and make du'a.

Prophet Muhammad ﷺ said it better than I ever will: *"Verily, one who does not hold anything from the Quran in his heart is like a ruined house."* And this doesn't mean having memorised it: it means welcoming its lessons and applying them, embracing the Divine words as guidance for us to obey our Creator, purify our intentions and soften our characters.

You might try absolutely everything: if Allah ﷻ has declared it, He won't make it happen. You know why? Because the one who doesn't *want* to change, will *never* change. It doesn't mean you failed at being their way out. You probably played a bigger part than you think. If not, it simply means this was another lesson for you to learn.

"INDEED, ALLAH ﷻ WILL NOT CHANGE THE CONDITION OF A PEOPLE UNTIL THEY CHANGE WHAT IS IN THEMSELVES."

(13:11)

THE PROPHET ﷺ SAID, "A SERVANT DOES NOT HAVE FAITH UNTIL HE BELIEVES IN DIVINE PROVIDENCE, BOTH ITS GOOD AND ITS HARM, AND UNTIL HE KNOWS THAT WHAT AFFLICTS HIM COULD NEVER HAVE MISSED HIM AND WHAT MISSED HIM COULD HAVE NEVER AFFLICTED HIM."

AL-TIRMIDHI 2144

Kindness

Our beloved Prophet ﷺ said, "*Allah ﷻ is Kind, and He loves kindness in all matters*" (Al Bukhari, 6528) but somehow, many have forgotten not only the importance of spreading kindness but also of appreciating it in a world that keeps getting darker everyday.

Growing up I was often being told that I was *too* kind, that people would take advantage of that and that I would keep getting hurt. Did it actually happen? Yes of course. Did I believe that it was a sign of weakness? Sometimes. Have I ever regretted it? Absolutely not. If anything, I genuinely think that this what made me stronger and say Alhamdulillah for it. I mean, why should I give up on this quality that He, *The Most Kind*, blessed me with? Aren't we supposed to be inspired by His names?

Here's a funny story I want to share with you: back when I was studying in Copenhagen, me and my friends decided to share what were the first impression of each other. One of them said: "At first I thought you were super fake because I don't trust people that are too kind. I thought it was suspicious." My old insecure yourself would have felt so bad about this and would have probably teared up but it actually made me laugh as her and I were pretty close at this point.

She then added "I realised after a few days that it was actually one of your qualities, that you genuinely cared about us and it really made me wonder how kind people make it through life honestly. People are reckless these days." To be fair, she might have been a little too pessimistic and I'm not sure kind people are actually that rare. Some people, because of their scars, just prefer to be kind with those they think deserve it. Others assume that it doesn't matter how the other person treats you, kindness is always the way to go.

I've learned that if you're not balanced, you end up being kind either to no one or to everyone but yourself. Putting others first and putting yourself last isn't more respectable in any way. When I reflect on my past experiences, it is obvious that it is what I did most of my life and interestingly enough, when I started protecting my peace or communicating on how I'd truly been feeling, I could tell it was unpleasant to a few. Now I know that those who feel this way were never kind enough to me in the first place and that I wasn't being fair to myself when tolerating that. So here's my advice to you: treat people like you want to be treated. Always be kind for the sake of Allah ﷻ. Simply remember that it doesn't mean letting people treat you like dirt. Your heart deserves to be held gently too.

THE PROPHET ﷺ SAID, "WHOEVER HAS THE QUALITY OF KINDNESS HAS BEEN GIVEN HIS SHARE OF GOODNESS. WHOEVER IS DEPRIVED OF THE QUALITY OF KINDNESS HAS BEEN DEPRIVED OF HIS SHARE OF GOODNESS."

AL TIRMIDHI, 2013

THE PROPHET ﷺ SAID,

"HE WHO IS DEPRIVED OF KINDNESS IS DEPRIVED OF GOODNESS."

MUSLIM, 2592

Doubt

Have you ever been through times where you weren't sure anymore if everything you'd been doing was actually being taken into consideration? Or that Allah ﷻ probably wasn't looking at you anymore because of all the times you've disobeyed His commands?

We all have our weaknesses, thoughts we wouldn't dare to share, sins we struggle to stop despite knowing how bad they are, flaws that don't align with the character a Muslim should have and that sometimes lead us to prioritise this dunya over our deen, to the point we're like *'ugh, I wish I could just do this'*, *'I wish it wasn't haram'* or *'what is the point of all of this?'*.

Luckily, Allah ﷻ knows and that's why He blessed us with the gem the Quran is. Anytime you're going through an existential crisis that makes you question your whole life and everything you sacrifice to please Him, His words shine as miracles. No matter which page you open, you see how it talks to your heart and makes any doubt you have disappear. I mean, we can all agree that the deeper you dive into it, the more obvious it is that it wasn't written by a human being. The Quran incarnates the *Tawhid* and reminds you of how we do not have to be flawless because only He is, so what is there to doubt about?

Remember this dunya is actually like a labyrinth. Sometimes you feel lost, like you're facing a wall, like you want to give up, but you're lucky enough to have the Quran as your guide, a compass for you heart to get out successfully.

Another possibility might be that you're not doubting Allah ﷻ but yourself. The thing is, even the best of us do. Think about the reaction of Prophet Muhammad ﷺ when he encountered Jibril (as) for the first time! He ran to Khadijah (ra) and was afraid he was losing his mind Subhan'Allah ﷻ.

Doubt will never mean you're not worthy of being Muslim. What it comes down to is the actions resulting from these thoughts, how you decide to deal with them. Stressing over having doubts is just like worrying about the purity of your intentions: if the seed of faith wasn't planted in your heart, you wouldn't even think about all of this. So again, the choice is up to you: will you take time to water it or let it die when the first signs of dryness appear?

We all have our weaknesses, thoughts we wouldn't dare to share, sins we struggle to stop despite knowing how bad they are, flaws that don't align with the character a Muslim should have and that sometimes lead us to prioritise this dunya over our deen, to the point we're like 'ugh, I wish I could just do this', 'I wish it wasn't haram', 'it can't be that wrong'…

Let me share a personal story here: growing up with non-muslim people around and being a romantic often led me to have these thoughts when I had a crush on someone. I was a pretty insecure and shy girl so I wouldn't get into it anyway (it turned out to be a blessing in disguise I guess haha!) yet I had felt like I would never cross any limits if that ever happened, that me hanging out with a boy I liked didn't have to imply being physical or talk about stuff you're only supposed to mention with your husband, that I loved Allah ﷻ enough to manage my self-control properly. It is only when I got older that He opened my eyes on these thoughts I had.

A few year ago I was living in London for my studies and had met this Muslim guy who seemed great on many points but was also very attractive. As usual, I had been very honest about my decision to preserve myself for marriage and do things the halal way, which he was pleasantly surprised by and initially respectful of. However, he knew that my family was in France, meaning that I could easily invite people over at my place. After a few days, he suggested visiting me after class.

I vividly remember my heart getting really tight when reading his message. Maybe he didn't have wrong intentions and may Allah ﷻ forgive him if he did, but I certainly was extremely upset by what I had just read. Did Sheytan whisper *'no one would know, and it doesn't mean anything will happen, you know your limits'*? Of course. But Subhan'Allah ﷻ it didn't feel right. The idea crossing my mind made me feel impure, as if I actually didn't really trust myself. I started tearing up and asked Allah ﷻ to forgive me for even simply being tempted by this.

Alhamdulillah looking back I think this is a sweet reaction and I'm proud I didn't let this happen but this enlightened me in many ways. These thoughts made me sick for a man that I had just met and didn't have feelings for yet — what if it'd had been someone I had let myself fall in love with?

If there's even the tiniest breach of doubt about something Allah ﷻ commanded, if your *nafs* is not convinced that a certain order is for your own good, then Sheytan is going to make it crack until you break, whatever this might be about. You can't overestimate yourself in a situation like this because the truth is, you can only have control to a certain extent. Even if you were an exception and actually managed to not give in, it doesn't mean that Allah ﷻ was proud of you for being so presumptuous about it and for being comfortable with it now. At the end of the day, you're still purposely putting yourself in a situation He dislikes and warned you about because you assume you know better than Him. Astaghfirullah.

I hope this shows you that we were all created the same way, and no matter how strong you believe your faith is, your nature as a human will catch up on you. If Prophet Adam (as) caved in, what makes you think you won't?

I know how overwhelming it can be sometimes, but this whole game that is life is not supposed to be easy for us. Think and act wisely sister.

THE PROPHET ﷺ SAID:

"LEAVE WHAT MAKES YOU IN DOUBT FOR WHAT DOES NOT MAKE YOU IN DOUBT. THE TRUTH BRINGS TRANQUILITY WHILE FALSEHOOD SOWS DOUBT."

AL-TIRMIDHI, 2518

"A COMPANION CAME TO HIM AND SAID: 'MESSENGER OF ALLAH ﷻ! WE HAVE THOUGHTS WHICH WE CANNOT DARE TALK ABOUT AND WE DO NOT LIKE THAT WE HAVE THEM OR TALK ABOUT THEM. HE SAID:
HAVE YOU EXPERIENCED THAT? THEY REPLIED: YES. HE SAID : THAT IS CLEAR FAITH.'"

ABI DAWUD 5111

Modesty

Modesty is way too often presented as a constraint for women and described as disrespectful to those who fought for being able to wear whatever they want or don't even have that choice. This kind of thought has always annoyed me, even before I started wearing hijab. I mean, why should we blame women who make the conscious choice to cover themselves for the fault of men who do not understand the concept of free will in Islam and therefore, feel entitled to force an act of worship on women? What is actually wrong with us not wanting to be defined by our bodies and prioritising our relationship to Allah ﷻ? Do they really believe that taking this right away from us will serve the cause they pretend to defend?

Sometimes I wonder if what's disturbing to these detractors is how we remind them of something that, deep down, they think could actually be the truth... When you think about it, hijab is more visible than praying 5 times a day, not drinking alcohol or not dating, and it isn't periodic like fasting during Ramadan. Consequently, you do represent Islam at all times. But why would the way we dress cause so much hate and anger, if it wasn't because of how it challenges their whole belief systems and egos?

You know, *al haya*, modesty, isn't just about covering for His sake and doesn't mean losing sight of your femininity : it actually uncovers your *true* beauty, the one from a heart that is filled with humility, piety and tawakkul. The one who might go against society's beauty standards but checks our Creator's.

Interestingly, even when I didn't wear hijab, I never felt comfortable with men solely being attracted by my physic. It didn't feel right. I loved the idea that my body was so precious that only a handful of people deserved to see it, but also, that if anyone was interested in me in the first place it would be because of my inner beauty, the one that gives me a special outer glow that goes beyond how pretty my hair or my curves look. And you know what? That's exactly what happened when I finally took the plunge. Non-Muslim people I've known for years have told me I look happier, more confident and brighter ever since I started wearing hijab. I feel so much more like myself ever since I started wearing it, almost as if I was feeling the *fitrah* Subhan'Allah ﷻ.

Social media often makes it feel like you can't share a caring reminder to a sister wearing certain things that are not really modest, or contrariwise, that there is only one correct way to wear it and anything else is not considered as hijab to eyes of Allah ﷻ. This is problematic on so many levels, not only because judgment and pride are involved, but also because it brings modesty and hijab to two extremes, one being too lax, and the other one being intransigent.

It is a journey for sure and it is okay to take it step by step, as long as you preserve your intentions and make sure they're all about pleasing Him rather than others, including yourself.

You know by now how important I think it is to be balanced, right in the middle, so here are my thoughts on this: make sure to question yourself and be open to improvement without ever claiming what you're doing is an example to follow, but don't make it a burden that is going to make you unhappy and regret your decision either. At the end of the day, Allah ﷻ knows our inner struggles and our journeys, and although we should be reminded of the true meaning of hijab, we should also make sure we show kindness and empathy towards each other.

Here are a few things we need to keep in mind:

- Dressing modestly might be considered disrespectful to some, but it is respectful to Allah ﷻ.
- Consequently, not only women but also men should be modest.
- No one should ever force a woman to wear something she does not wish to wear. You may advise gently, make du'a and leave the rest to Him.
- Beauty standards are worthless if you're not beautiful to Allah ﷻ.
- Hijab empowers you in ways you never thought were possible when you truly connect to its meaning and embrace it.
- Every pious women wears hijab but not every hijabi is pious. Hijab is an obligation, but it doesn't make you irreproachable or infallible. Don't put hijabi on a pedestal.
- Nothing will make you more beautiful than the softness of your heart and the sincerity of your faith.

The Prophet ﷺ said, "Verily, every religion has a character and the character of Islam is modesty."

Sunan Ibn Majah 4182

The Prophet ﷺ said, "Modesty (al-haya) is a branch of faith."

Sunan an-Nasa'i 5004

The Prophet ﷺ said, "Vulgarity is not found in anything but that it disgraces it, and modesty is not found in anything but that it beautifies it."

Al-Tirmidhi 1974

Womanhood

Being a woman in this life can be tough at times, let alone being a Muslim woman.

You know, I feel extremely fortunate that my father (may Allah ﷻ bless him) treated us the way he did. He always made us feel special, not only as daughters, but as young Muslimas. He encouraged us to study, to discover the world, to believe in ourselves all while sticking to our values. He was also my mom's best friend and to us, they were an actual *team*.

This means that I've always found it deeply saddening to see certain people act like all we must do is being submissive to the men in our lives, shutting our dreams down, neglecting ourselves and feeling worthless. Women believing that's just how things are and that we should simply accept it is even more heartbreaking.

This isn't what Islam teaches whatsoever. In fact, Abu Huraira reported that our beloved Prophet Muhammad ﷺ said: "The most complete of the believers in faith are those with the best character, and the best of you are the best in behaviour to their women." (Al-Tirmidhi 1162)

He used to have so much respect for women and a lot of admiration for His first wife, Khadija bint Khuwaylid (ra). There wasn't a day he didn't mention her until he passed away. He constantly felt honoured by her love, was impressed by her success and intelligence, humbled by how such a powerful lady would consider marrying a simple shepherd like him. He saw her as an actual life partner, as his lover, his best friend and his family. He knew how valuable she was and never treated her as his servant. He never defined her by who she'd been married to. He loved her for who *she was*, not just for what *she was giving*.

So, what happened to us? Why is there still so much unhealthy ego wars and iniquity between men and women when Allah ﷻ has given us specific roles and created us in pairs? We keep criticising the Western world on these matters but we also failed to follow the precepts of our deen accordingly.

Please never think that Allah ﷻ wants anyone to treat us like empty souls who are not supposed to have any ambition, any education, any hobby. Of course we, as women, have duties that we cannot ignore, but we also were blessed with so many rights that show how precious we are to The Greatest. Therefore, you should focus on those who see your wins as theirs, who love you so deeply they won't be content unless you blossom into the best version of yourself.

Muslim women are amazing. They're entrepreneurs, activists, athletes, chefs, architects, doctors, scientists. They're lawyers, queens, creatives, journalists, psychologists, engineers, teachers and so much more. Their identities are just as diverse as nature, yet they all have one thing in common: being diamonds to Allah ﷻ.

Some assume that we cannot achieve these goals all while being caring daughters, wives and mothers. Others think that decisions like wearing hijab or staying at home to raise a family rather than getting a job means you were necessarily forced to do so, that you are submissive to men, that you are illiterate, that being Muslim means we will simply never be able to speak our voices because our religion is all about oppression. They're all pretty much underestimating how strong and resilient Allah ﷻ made us.

It is essential for us and future generations to build solid support systems. There is no need for constant competition, comparison, backbiting or judgement, there is enough space for all of us to shine. As Muslim women, we can relate to each other, learn from each other, find comfort in each other. Our experiences, the way we feel and navigate life, the way our bodies work are things that men will never be able to comprehend and therefore will never be able to address properly. There's a better way for us to celebrate womanhood according to Islamic principles and it starts with our friendships, with how we raise our daughters, with the way we communicate, behave and show respect not only to Allah ﷻ, to men, to each other, but also, to ourselves.

Being a Muslimah will never mean you must neglect yourself. Be feminine, be soft, be mindful of the way you speak, of the places you visit, of the people you surround yourself with. Take care of yourself as you would take care of your most precious piece of jewellery.

THE PROPHET ﷺ SAID:

"TREAT WOMEN WELL, FOR WOMAN IS CREATED FROM A RIB AND THE MOST CURVED PORTION OF THE RIB IS ITS UPPER PORTION. IF YOU TRY TO STRAIGHTEN IT, IT WILL BREAK, BUT IF YOU LEAVE IT AS IT IS, IT WILL REMAIN CURVED. SO TREAT WOMEN WITH KINDNESS."

AL BUKHARI 3153

"AND LIVE WITH THEM IN KINDNESS. FOR IF YOU DISLIKE THEM - PERHAPS YOU DISLIKE A THING AND ALLAH ﷻ MAKES THEREIN MUCH GOOD."

(4:19)

Resilience

I thought about 20 year old me and what I would tell her if I met her today. I hate to admit it, but all the things that came to my mind first were the things I didn't accomplish and things that I'm currently struggling with.

But as my mom (bless her and may she forgive me for being so hard on myself at times) said, what about all the things I did accomplish? What about all the things I did with right intentions, the sacrifices I made for Allah ﷻ? And she's right.

I need to remind myself that the reward of the Akhirah is far better than any one I can get in this dunya, that my efforts, my resilience and patience through it all will never go unnoticed to Allah ﷻ. My life might not look like what I expected for myself or what we usually expect from an almost 30 year old woman — but it's okay, because behind all of this, there has been a soul working really hard, who persevered to hold onto her deen and to take with her all the good she did, not the worldly things she achieved.

When you accumulate trials in the different spheres of your life (family, career, health, relationships...), it can really take a toll on you and impact your relationship with Allah ﷻ. You might also beat yourself up because you keep failing the same tests over and over again, even when you asked Allah ﷻ to relieve you from it or had all the intention to not fail again.

We don't understand everything that happens to us, and we need to recognise that these things are over our control. It was simply written that way. This dunya is hard. It is what it is, and *sabr* in that case is not about patience but truly about resilience in the face of complexity.

I just want you to know that frustration and sadness are normal reactions. You're only human and you're allowed to feel the way you feel. There's so much stigma around mental health and dealing with your emotions when it is so necessary to do so in order to move forward and grow.

Remember: He doesn't burden a soul beyond that it can bear. This means He knows your ability to show resilience through it all. After all, He gives the toughest battles to His strongest soldiers, right?

He knows you can overcome the pain and guilt. He wants you to learn. He wants you to grow and most importantly, He is giving you signs and chances to go back to Him. The more He loves you, the more He will test you because He know how humans are when they get everything they want, He know how we will prioritise everything but our relationship with Him.

So don't let the outcome of these tests take control over your whole life and precious time. Muslims were given the Quran as a cure for the hearts. We were blessed with so much light, let's not drown ourselves in darkness.

"AND WE WILL SURELY TEST YOU WITH SOMETHING OF FEAR AND HUNGER AND A LOSS OF WEALTH AND LIVES AND FRUITS, BUT GIVE GOOD TIDINGS TO THE PATIENT,"

(2:155)

"AND STRIVE FOR ALLAH ﷻ WITH THE STRIVING DUE TO HIM. HE HAS CHOSEN YOU AND HAS NOT PLACED UPON YOU IN THE RELIGION ANY DIFFICULTY."

(22:78)

Forgiveness

I think we underestimate the power and beauty of forgiveness Subhan'Allah ﷻ.

So many people message me saying they're too ashamed to do their Salah so they give up on it. If you tell yourself *'how can I stand in front of Allah ﷻ after disobeying Him so much'*, *'I don't deserve to make du'a'*, *'I don't have that connection to Salah'*, just have a look at the 99 names of Allah ﷻ and reflect upon all His qualities. The way Islam was taught to you might have led you to only picture Him as The Punisher. Although we shouldn't underestimate His wrath, He is so much more than that. He is the Forgiver and loves to forgive. Therefore, your limiting beliefs about Allah ﷻ need to disappear so your bond to Him remains unbreakable, even when this life breaks you.

Salah is one of the most important pillars of Islam for a reason. It is the foundation on which you build your imaan. If it's not there and stable, nothing will hold together.

I'm not saying being always completely dedicated to your Salah is easy, but you absolutely need it. It is your main bond to our Creator, please don't break it. He literally gave us 5 opportunities a day to talk to *Him*. This number used to be 50, because He knew we would fail at obeying Him at all times. Yet, He accepted to decrease that number because He also knew we would never keep up, but didn't decrease His Mercy with it.

Allah ﷻ doesn't need Salah. *We do.* Its purpose isn't just to worship Him and ask for what we wish for, but also to purify ourselves and lift the burdens of our mistakes.

We all sin. Even the Prophets (as) did for God sake! We struggle with getting up to pray at times, having *sabr*, managing anger or putting Allah ﷻ first. Your struggles show you're human, but acknowledging them shows that you care and that you have it all in your heart. Don't be hard on yourself or think you're not worthy of asking for forgiveness. If you make one step towards Allah ﷻ, He'll make ten steps towards you. If you walk towards Him, He'll run towards you.

Prophet Dawud (as) said, *"What is the most refreshing?"* To which Prophet Suleyman (as) said, *"That Allah ﷻ forgives people and people forgive each other."* (Tafsīr Ibn Abi Hatim (38:30)). I think this is so true and beautiful.

I've personally always found it easier to forgive others than myself, but I do understand how hard forgiving someone can be at times. When you gave so much, feel deeply hurt or betrayed, it can be incredibly challenging to let go of those feelings, even more so when you don't even get any apologies. When you invested so much trust in someone, only to be disappointed or wronged, the wounds they inflicted may run deep, leaving scars that might take years to heal.

I've been there and I still find it unfair at times. I mean yes, saying 'I'm sorry' means setting your ego aside and admitting fault, but sometimes even that isn't enough to erase the pain they've caused or the damage they've inflicted. It can be frustrating to see them move on after uttering those words (or worse, not even doing so) while we're left grappling with the aftermath of their actions.

However I now know that holding onto grudges only burdens your heart and that it doesn't matter if people aren't fair to you because Allah ﷻ, the One who matters the most, will always be.

Choosing to forgive might take time. It requires acknowledging the pain while also recognising the humanity of the person who caused it. It means learning to not let unanswered questions overflow your mind and burn your heart anymore. Most importantly, it isn't about condoning or forgetting what happened; rather, it's about releasing the grip of resentment and choosing to move forward. It is an act of strength that ultimately leads to inner peace because you accept that things were written that way, that your principles and values might not be as universal as you thought they were and that you need these experiences to grow.

And same goes for your own self you know? Forgiving yourself demands facing your past mistakes and flaws with no harsh judgment but with compassion and eventually, relief. You don't need to feel unworthy of forgiveness and remain mad at yourself for the things you genuinely regret: if Allah ﷻ forgave you for that, why wouldn't you?

"AND WHOEVER IS PATIENT AND FORGIVES - INDEED, THAT IS OF THE MATTERS [REQUIRING] DETERMINATION."

(42:43)

"SAY, O MY SERVANTS WHO HAVE TRANSGRESSED AGAINST THEMSELVES [BY SINNING], DO NOT DESPAIR OF THE MERCY OF ALLAH ﷻ. INDEED, ALLAH ﷻ FORGIVES ALL SINS. INDEED, IT IS HE WHO IS THE FORGIVING, THE MERCIFUL."

(39:53)

Introspection

Ego is always gonna be your worst enemy. In fact, it can be scarier than the influence of Sheytan.

One should never assume they don't need advice or to be reminded of anything, especially coming from someone who might not look or be as practising. Likewise, one shouldn't overly use the argument of '*Allah ﷻ knows what is in my heart*' to justify not obeying Him. Islam is a religion of norms, not exceptions, which means that we have guidelines to follow, sacred words that were gifted to us as a reminder of what goodness and steadfastness look like for Muslims.

We can't minimise the impact of our actions just because our intentions are pure according to our own perception — because yes, that is also something we need to challenge consistently to make sure we haven't convince ourselves that whatever we're thinking was in fact not that alarming. For example, if you drink alcohol every now and then, you cannot claim that your intentions aren't wrong because you never cross the lign of being unconscious of your actions; if you decide to get a tattoo, you cannot say that Allah ﷻ will understand because it has a cultural and personal meaning to you. Committing the sin, exposing it and downplaying its gravity is worse than committing it and admitting you'd been weak.

I remember this one time I was at the mosque for Jumm'ah. We'd just finished praying when suddenly, a heated argument between two sisters happened. One of them was older and I heard her say *"Who do you think you are to tell me this? I performed Hajj when you don't even wear hijab, you better keep quiet."* To this day, it is one of the most shocking and unpleasant experiences I've had with the community, and even more so, in one of the houses of Allah ﷻ (may He guide us all).

Appreciating your worth as a Muslimah should never come with despising others or not giving the benefit of the doubt to someone who might simply care for you. There's enough space for us to shine together and encourage each other to become better, but for that we truly need to challenge our *nafs* and confront everything that holds us back from embracing unity and compassion. It is harder to acknowledge our own shortcomings than point out others' flaws for sure, but by setting aside our pride, we can not only build bridges instead of walls in the Ummah, but also, evolve as individuals.

May Allah ﷻ purify our hearts and fill them with peace, kindness and sincerity in everything that we do.

Sister, here's an important reminder for you: the momentary pleasures, the minimum efforts, the denial, the neglect and complacency will never serve you. Let's say you've been making a du'a consistently for a long time and have yet to see it being granted, or maybe you're seeing no way out to the issues you've been facing for a while. I understand how nerve-wracking this might be, but have you ever wondered *why*?

Before questioning Him, make sure to ask yourself if you've been doing what needs to be done. How's the quality of your salah? How's your relationship with your parents? Is your income halal? Are your intentions pure?

It isn't just about waiting patiently for things to happen, it's about building tawakkul, challenging yourself and doing your part. Nurture your trust in Him and seize the opportunities He gives you, stop thinking they do not exist. Open your mind and heart to His signs. Have this urge to welcome and deal with your negative thoughts in a mindful yet determined way until the first thing that comes to your mind when things don't go how you'd like is saying Alhamdulillah.

When Allah ﷻ decides something for you that is different from what you expected, say Alhamdulillah a thousand times because His choice is always going to be a thousand times better than yours.

"NEVER HAVE I DEALT WITH ANYTHING MORE DIFFICULT THAN MY OWN SOUL, WHICH SOMETIMES HELPS ME AND SOMETIMES OPPOSES ME."

AL GHAZALI

THE PROPHET ﷺ SAID:
"THE STRONG ARE NOT THOSE WHO DEFEAT PEOPLE. RATHER, THE STRONG ARE THOSE WHO DEFEAT THEIR OWN EGO."

IBN HIBBAN 717

Community

Do you ever think about how beautiful and special the way we greet each other is? Subhan'Allah ﷻ, He truly put signs in the simplest things.

You know, sometimes I wonder how the monsters who uses the sacred name of The Almighty to justify committing atrocities believe they're on The Right Path. I mean, are they not aware of the meaning and essence of *Assalamu Aleykum?* Do they prepare by saying *Bismillah Ar-Rahman Ar-Rahim* when the saying encompasses the endless Love, Mercy and Kindness of Allah ﷻ who wants us to have these traits? I'm not even talking about complicated things, just again, the simplest ones. Yet it's like the ashes they leave behind keep blinding them and darkening their hearts.

While they bare the responsibility of the hate towards our deen, we know that they actually have nothing to do with us. This is not, and will never be Islam, because its soul is right in the middle. It is all about balance.

We live in a world that, although it is getting better, still somehow pushes us to be in an unhealthy competition with each other. You see certain men treating us with so much disrespect, feeling untitled to criticise as if they were absolutely irreproachable, women being unhappy for the success of their sisters, being envious of who they get married to, assuming they're better muslims, and just do not consider their peers with care and kindness.

However, isn't us building brotherhood and sisterhood a way to be stronger? Honestly, I think Prophet Muhammad ﷺ would be so disappointed to see how we've been treating each other. As someone who dedicated his life and gave up everything to build a community of Muslims, it would've been so heartbreaking for him to witness the state of the Ummah at times. I mean there's a reason why we call each other *brothers and sisters*. We are supposed to be like a *family* and I think we can all agree we don't always feel this way, especially on social media.

You know, one of my friends who's a revert once told me: *"I love Islam, but I hate the Ummah"* and I couldn't even blame her for it, but I still hope and pray that despite our flaws, we can strive for unity and respect to eventually embody the true spirit of Islam.

"AND IT IS THUS THAT WE APPOINTED YOU TO BE THE COMMUNITY OF THE MIDDLE WAY SO THAT YOU MIGHT BE WITNESSES TO ALL MANKIND AND THE MESSENGER MIGHT BE A WITNESS TO YOU."

(2:143)

"THE BELIEVERS ARE BUT BROTHERS, SO MAKE SETTLEMENT BETWEEN YOUR BROTHERS. AND FEAR ALLAH ﷻ THAT YOU MAY RECEIVE MERCY."

(49:10)

Humility

You know, my teenage years were pretty bad. In fact, I felt miserable. Whenever I read my 2007-2009 diaries, it breaks my heart seeing everything that was going on in my head yet not sharing it with anyone but myself. I think there was a part of me who felt ashamed, but I was also convinced that no one needed to know what I was struggling with. They were my own issues that I needed to solve and shouldn't bother anyone with.

Luckily, *Salah* already held an important place in my heart back then. I would pour my heart out to Allah ﷻ, crying so much in *sujood*, sharing my saddest thoughts and how much I needed Him to help me. You know, the deep sense of comfort and relief you get when you concentrate, look down, come to the ground and prostrate is unmatchable, but also, a beautiful act of humility. It makes you feel so small and vulnerable yet so empowered and light.

While I do still feel the same way about praying, I've had to improve at asking for help to others, as I've realised this is also what humility is about.

See, Allah ﷻ didn't create you so you would navigate life by yourself. Sure our environments might sometimes be unhealthy and you might have been deceived by some who didn't care about you as much as you cared about them, who betrayed your trust and made it look like you didn't deserve to be heard. I've been there and I know exactly how it feels to be told you're too sensitive, that you take things too personally, that you need to toughen up and that these things shouldn't hurt you. Hearing this turned me into someone who thought she always had to have it together, that being vulnerable meant being weak and who regretted every time she opened up to someone a little bit too much.

It took me years to deconstruct all of this and accept that my feelings are valid, that if I loved being a source of hope and trust to others, then it wasn't fair to deprive someone else from that joy. I also was depriving myself from witnessing compassion and humanity, bonding moments that would turn into precious memories. I didn't want my ego to make me believe I was among the few to be trustworthy anymore and realised that on that specific aspect, I wasn't as humble as I should have.

If our beloved Prophet ﷺ, saw some of his closest people refusing to follow His message and hurt him, yet still had companions and wives he confided in and trusted, don't you think you can give people a chance to be a light in *your* life too?

And if contrariwise, you haven't been relying on Allah ﷻ when facing challenges or sometimes wonder if He's actually listening, read this carefully:

You need to be humble enough to recognise that things will always be hard if you deal with them through anyone but Him. The fact you're tired yet keep holding onto His rope is a beautiful proof of faith He will never ignore. He is the only one who He will never let you down, who will never get bored of you repeating the same things over and over again, whatever time it may be and despite already knowing absolutely everything going on in your head.

Talk to Him. Ask for forgiveness for thinking you could figure it out without consulting Him first. Work on your Salah, it is called a pillar for a reason: just like a house cannot be built without stable foundations, your imaan cannot grow without a stable, sincere Salah.

Besides, don't you think there's something incredibly peaceful and reassuring about praying and watching someone pray? The way we lower our heads with humility and whisper to our Creator... It's so unique and life changing. So, make it a moment in your day to look forward to, tell yourself you're meeting with your Best Friend, measure the honour it is to be called to stand in prayer and be grateful for being reminded of how small yet special you are to Him.

The aya on the next page always blows my mind and profoundly touched me the first time I read it.

We are currently more than 8 billion people on Earth, and Allah ﷻ knows absolutely everything about everyone: He knows what we are all thinking at every second, why we act the way we do and how our whole lives are going to unfold. He knows us better than we know ourselves. And if these knowledge — which is only a small part of everything that He knows Subhan'Allah ﷻ — had to be written down, it would only make sense that the sea would never be enough.

When I think about it, the sea seems so immense and overwhelming, and in comparison, a few pens would probably be enough to write what I know... So how could I possibly even dare to compete with Him when it comes to deciding what is good for me?

This is a lesson of humility, but also an invitation from Him. An invitation to reflect upon the things He has decided and take them as opportunities to strengthen our trust in His plan. Because at the end of the day, everything is and happens for a reason, and the closer we are to Him, the more likely we will be to appreciate that and calm our hearts.

"NOTHING IS DIFFICULT WHEN YOU SEEK IT THROUGH YOUR LORD AND NOTHING IS EASY WHEN YOU SEEK IT THROUGH YOURSELF."

AHMAD IBN 'ATA ALLAH ﷺ

"IF THE SEA WERE INK FOR [WRITING] THE WORDS OF MY LORD, THE SEA WOULD BE EXHAUSTED BEFORE THE WORDS OF MY LORD WERE EXHAUSTED, EVEN IF WE BROUGHT THE LIKE OF IT AS A SUPPLEMENT."

(18:109)

Discipline

Growing up, a lot of people have been surprised by how I've managed to have so much discipline in the practice of my deen in a non-Muslim country, surrounded by non-Muslim friends and colleagues. As grateful to Allah ﷻ as I am for this, I have to admit that the temptation of indulging to certain worldly pleasures was high, and I sometimes felt frustrated for choosing to be this disciplined (and Alhamdulillah, here I'm not saying 'having to' because I wasn't doing it for my parents or anyone else, but out of choice).

I knew that those sacrifices would contribute to my ticket to Jannah in some ways but didn't really dig into it. Besides, you know how it is, right? How the *waswas* of Shaytan and your *nafs* can trick you into thinking that acting upon your desires would make your life so much better, that pne mistake won't mean much in the grand scheme of things even if Allah ﷻ is watching… But then reality catches up on you and you feel like you're betraying Him because you know He doesn't want this, He doesn't expect this from you.

So you ended up resisting *for His Sake*.

But the truth is, even if this has saved you from caving in many times, it might not always be the case.

We are selfish creatures and therefore, doing something for His sake only without understanding the interest behind it, only because He ordered you to might not always prevent you from disobedience, no matter how much you love and fear disappointing Him.

However doing it for *yourself* because you want to benefit from how good it is for you is different. It naturally makes it easier to have discipline, but also humbles you. Indeed, Allah ﷻ is the Satisfier of Needs: He loves it when you worship Him, but He certainly doesn't need anything from you. You are doing this for yourself only.

Sure the way Islam is usually taught doesn't necessarily give a profound meaning to this discipline we're supposed to have in our everyday lives. We are all familiar with the overused '*this is haram*' narrative with no explanation allowing us to welcome His commands with conviction or to delve deeper into the wisdom behind these teachings, when this is in fact the key to foster a genuine connection with our Creator and His guidance. May He make it easy for us.

I was lucky enough to witness this from afar, as my parents didn't have this approach with us Alhamdulillah, yet in hindsight, I believe that my lack of maturity and personal spiritual education were the main cause of it all. I was aware of the fact that the things forbidden in Islam are prohibited as a means for us to please Him (resisting the pleasures of this dunya for the sake of The One we don't see does deserve a reward after all). However, I never thought of them as a protection because they wouldn't benefit us neither in this dunya nor in the Akhirah.

Nowadays, many studies show the dangers of eating pork, how unhealthy even small quantities of alcohol are, how common STD have become, how addicting gambling can be to only name a few... All those things that Allah ﷻ has preserved us from Subhan'Allah ﷻ.

I guess they serve as umpteenth proof of His love for us Alhamdulillah.

You know, this life is a test, and just like any test, you try, you stumble, you fall, you get up and you try again until you get it right. In fact, one thing that I like to remind myself is that practicing Islam is very much like exercising.

Sometimes you feel lazy and completely unmotivated; sometimes it becomes so hard that it makes you cry, but there is never a moment when you actually regret doing it because deep down, you know how good it is for you and you can feel it right after. Discipline and consistency are what transform it into a healthy habit you can't live without anymore.

And just as you shouldn't overexercise or neglect the rights your body has on you, you need to be balanced and mindful in the way you practice self-discipline. In this life, we get tested in two different ways: through the things we can control, and the ones we can't. You need to let go of the latter.

Only then will you realise that Islam isn't difficult; humans have made it seem this way and your worst enemy in all of this is always going to be *yourself*.

The more you nurture your love for Allah ﷻ, the easier it will be for you 1. to let go of things that might give momentary pleasure but lead to a lifetime of regret and 2. accepting what He's written for you.

Likewise, the more you leave the things that harden your heart, the easier it'll be for you to love, trust and obey Him.

Self-discipline, therefore, becomes just another expression of self-love for His sake.

Things you can control

- Your imaan
- Your character
- Your intentions
- Your knowledge
- Your modesty
- Your speech
- Your actions
- Your self-care
- Your company
- Your time

Things you can't control

- People's thoughts
- People's actions
- People's feelings
- Illness and health issues
- Unexpected challenges
- Injustice in this world
- The Qadr of Allah ﷻ
- The Future
- The Past
- Death

"But as for he who feared the position of his Lord and prevented the soul from [unlawful] inclination,

Then indeed, Paradise will be [his] refuge."

(79:40-41)

"Your nafs is just like your enemy, once it finds you serious, it obeys you. If it finds weakness from you, it will take you as a prisoner."

Ibn Al Qayyim

Purpose

If you're like me, you most likely feel like your purpose is to make people's lives better. From a young age, I've always loved solving problems, being that person you can confide to and who can help you out as much as possible. This, in addition to being the oldest child, led people in every area of my life to rely on me a lot and see me as the one you seek help from and ask for advice. I mean, I think you can tell this even now with the page — I genuinely love people and thrive from being helpful to others.

My trustworthiness has always been one of my qualities I cherished the most Alhamdulillah. Yet, I've noticed that overtime, my love for helping people turned into a need to save them. The empathy has reach a point where I want to relieve them from their pain, without considering the one I'm already bearing myself or whether they actually want that or not. This also means that whenever I feel like someone doesn't trust me enough/doesn't want to let me save them, I feel frustrated, burned out. I feel like I failed.

This isn't healthy, this isn't balanced, this isn't what I want, and most importantly, this isn't what Allah ﷻ wants from us. Allah ﷻ is Al Muhaymin, The Guardian, The All Controller, The Protector. You're not, I'm not, He is.

So while you should of course help others, it should never be at the cost of your own mental health and peace of heart. Setting these boundaries doesn't decrease your worth or mean you're giving up on anyone. It doesn't question your loyalty or sincerity in any ways, it doesn't make you less of a good person and in fact, doing this doesn't make you better than other either you might actually know how to help in a mindful way that doesn't imply neglecting themselves.

When you dig a little deeper into the why, you might even notice that your goal has never been to please Allah ﷻ through healing people but rather to avoid facing your own scars and heal yourself.

You know, I was reflecting upon my life and really couldn't imagine how it would have been if I wasn't Muslim. How I would have bared to witness so much hate and injustice between people, how I would have overcome this life's challenges, how I would have found a purpose... And to be completely honest, I'm not even sure I would have been able to do any of these.

It's so heartbreaking to see how Islam has been depicted over the past few years and to see so many Muslims drifting away from it, all because they think our deen will only deprive them from life enjoyment and love. I just wish they would see how it is truly 'a sea of hopes, a shore for the prettiest dreams', a way for us to give a deep spiritual meaning to our lives when most people only care about how much they will own and how many boxes of the society standards list they'll be able to tick.

Besides, your purpose in this life is so much bigger than all of this. Being a means through which people become better is amazing, but isn't it a little bit sad to only limit the reason of your existence to this? What about your personal relationship with Allah ﷻ? The other aspects of your character? He chose you to be part of the Ummah, to walk on the footsteps of our beloved Prophet ﷺ.

Let's make it a point to preserve our souls by increasing our trust in the power of du'as, in the Qadr of Allah ﷻ and in our ability to achieve great things.

Please take a step back and a moment to appreciate how whenever we struggle in this dunya, whenever it all feels a little pointless and empty, we have a rope to hold onto that reminds us, minuscule creatures that we are compared to the immensity of the universe, the true purpose of our existence. Most humans don't have that. In fact, 8 billion people on Earth and Allah ﷻ chose us to be Muslim. Doesn't that open your eyes on how valuable you are, the light you can radiate and the kind of mark you can leave behind?

And that doesn't mean you can't have goals in this dunya that are meaningful to you. As a matter of fact, you can be successful both in this life *and* the after one, as long as you never lose track of your bigger purpose in everything you undertake. You'll find that this will not only prevent you from feeling lost, but also, make you feel proud for finally learning to detach yourself from this worldly life while still appreciating what it has to offer.

"AND HE FOUND YOU LOST AND GUIDED [YOU]"

(93:7)

"DID YOU THINK THAT WE HAD CREATED YOU IN PLAY (WITHOUT ANY PURPOSE) AND THAT YOU WOULD NOT BE BROUGHT BACK TO US?"

(23:115)

"I HAVE CREATED THE JINN AND HUMANKIND ONLY FOR MY WORSHIP."

(51:56)

Sincerity

Today is one of these days where I feel numb thinking of how hard this dunya can be sometimes for those with a genuine soul, those who feel content with little, who give without expecting to receive, who listen without just waiting for their turn to talk, who can't help but gifting their whole hearts knowing too well not everyone is ready or wants to receive that amount of love.

These souls are like bees. The more time passes by, the rarer they are. They're essential to this world, but most are ungrateful to them. They won't do any or much harm, but most reject them. They take something good and turn it into something precious, but most forget about them.

The only times they're noticed are either when they sting because they didn't feel safe anymore, or when they're on the ground, exhausted from having done so much. The only times they're noticed are when they show you you've hurt them or when you realize you might lose them forever.

You might be the kindest, most devoted and calming person to someone and they'll still choose torments, pain and darkness. And they might be the roughest, most blinded person, you'll still see the light and hope in them.

They don't see that you, with grace and faith, touched their fragile soul without breaking them. You, just like the bees, can allow them to grow and bloom into the most beautiful version of themselves.

Please don't be mad at them for being scared of you just like people are scared of bees. If Allah ﷻ gave such a great mission to such a small creature, imagine the one He gave you.

"FOR THOSE WHO DO GOOD IN THIS WORLD IS GOOD; AND THE HOME OF THE HEREAFTER IS BETTER. AND HOW EXCELLENT IS THE HOME OF THE RIGHTEOUS"

(16:30)

THE PROPHET ﷺ SAID, "O ALLAH ﷻ, MAKE WHAT IS WITHIN ME BETTER THAN MY OUTWARD APPEARANCE AND MAKE MY OUTWARD APPEARANCE RIGHTEOUS. O ALLAH ﷻ, I ASK YOU FOR THE RIGHTEOUSNESS OF WHAT YOU GIVE TO PEOPLE OF PROPERTY, FAMILY, AND CHILDREN WITHOUT BEING MISGUIDED OR MISGUIDING OTHERS."

AL-TIRMIDHI 3586

Confidence

Recently, someone asked me how I got so confident and how I've successfully detached myself from people's opinion. So I thought I would share with you a little story.

A few years ago, one of my university classmate got a panic attack during her presentation. She spent the rest of the remaining time crying so I thought I would check on here at the end.

She opened up saying she hated this type of exercise and feeling like everybody was watching her. She then proceeded to add "*I wish it was as natural as you, you seem pretty confident.*"

I couldn't believe what she had just said and was literally too stunned to speak. Me? Confident? This had to be the craziest thing someone ever said about me, especially within the context of oral presentation. I mean yes, I had worked on myself but I didn't expect someone to be so positive about it.

Public speaking has always been a nightmare for me. It took me years and, as cliché as it sounds, a lot of 'fake it until you make it' and getting out of my comfort zone not to stop in the middle of a sentence and say *'I'm sorry I have to pause, I'm a little nervous'* with my hands holding my notes shaking as if it was -20°C. To this day, I forget how to breathe properly whenever I have to deliver a speech, but I've significantly improved Alhamdulillah.

When I shared that with her, she was so surprised because she couldn't tell I was nervous at all. She was also relieved that she wasn't the only one freaking out about this and hopeful for her to actually get better at it. She then wanted to know how I did it exactly.

The summer before this school year, I traveled to Indonesia for a month with a brand project in mind. I didn't know anyone there and thought that this would be pretty effective to build self-confidence (to be fair, you don't actually need to travel this far to work on yourself, I'm just a little crazy haha!).

You know, I forced myself to work on my fears because I hated feeling this way. The entrepreneurship lover that I was so impressed by these eloquent founders who knew how to keep our attention through compelling stories. Same goes with our prophets who were able to dismantle centuries old belief systems for the sake of Allah ﷻ. That had become one of my goals: I wanted people to listen to what I had to say.

So, here's the moment that changed my public speaking game forever: only a few days after landing in Bali, I attended a networking workshop with other young entrepreneurs and digital nomads. During this event, we were asked to randomly pick a piece of paper and do a one minute pitch about whatever was written. When it was my turn, I felt the familiar rush of anxiety coming and my heart racing. I took a deep breath, chose a paper and read this:

"Why is the sky blue?"

I'm not sure what crossed my mind when I discovered the prompt but Subhan'Allah ﷻ, not only did I know the scientific answer to it but I also felt the urge to address it from a religious perspective. I said *Bismillah* and started my pitch in front of 30 complete strangers.

When what felt like the longest minute of my life finally passed, I got their feedback and couldn't believe it: they listened *and* loved it. Did they notice I was nervous? Yes to a certain extent, but that didn't prevent them from actually thoroughly enjoy the pitch and ask more questions about my spirituality. I was ecstatic and thankful to Allah ﷻ for this experience which not only allowed me to get constructive feedback to improve, but also, to realise all it took for me was to say *Bismillah* and do my part with pure intentions. I felt different and for the first, confident.

It's important to note that it was never about doubting my knowledge or comparing it to others, which might also be a reason for feeling insecure. Having always been one of the "smart kids", I knew that my words could be valuable. The problem was about who was saying them.

For years I had o confidence in my appearance to the point I didn't even think a man would ever be romantically interested in me. I told myself that if I was skinnier, if I was prettier, then people would surely listen... Unless I compensated all of that with overachieving and leaving no space for mistakes. And guess what? That's what I did most of my life.

All it took to break my confidence was me standing in front of my class as a teenager and hearing some classmates yet again mocking my curves. I couldn't take it anymore and bursted into tears during my presentation. It was already hard enough for the shy, introverted 15 year old girl that I was to do this exercise, let alone being openly bullied by people who I didn't even know. I told myself that I never wanted to go through this type of humiliation ever again.

We also generally don't really picture leaders as introverts and naively think that extroverts are more confident. Before that trip to Indonesia, I thought I needed to change that part of me, and I did in a way. Don't get me wrong, I genuinely love people, insightful conversations and creating memories (can you tell my main love language is quality time?), but like any other introverted person, I need alone time to recharge.

For years, I acted like I had become extroverted who would never stop seeing people. The reality was that I would go home and be completely gut-wrenched from all these social interactions, just like when I had to speak in front of my class. I would subconsciously crave to be alone for days, but wouldn't allow myself to recharge, to not be a social person anymore. I owed it to my younger self to get out there and "shine" through my personality. I thought it would make people and myself forget about everything I didn't like about myself. They in fact didn't care, and I didn't forget.

It wasn't until I created The Mizaan and made Islam the center of my life that I realised all I had been doing didn't make any sense. I should have never assumed that my confidence solely relied on others' perception of me and that I needed to neglect my health just so I could prove myself that I was a good person, that I deserved self-love. Besides, true self confidence cannot come from the validation of the creatures, but only of the Creator's and one of the most precious lessons He taught me is that the more I place my trust in Him, the more confident I feel Subhan'Allah ﷻ.

Know that that the right people for you will always encourage you to learn and grow all while making you feel secure about who you are. They will never feel threatened by you or claim that the sole purpose of your existence is to please a man, to fit into a mould, to follow a certain path or to look a certain way.

You want to be a housewife? Beautiful. You want to launch a small business? Wonderful. You value education and want to pursue your studies? Fantastic. You prefer to spend time at home rather than seeing friends every weekend? Good for you! All of this is just one facet of your identity. You are so much more than that, and even more so to the eyes of Allah ﷻ. As long as you never compromise on your relationship with Him and yourself, then you truly have nothing to worry about.

"THE ONES WHO OFFER THEIR HEARTS TO ALLAH ﷻ, NEITHER THE ABSENCE NOR PRESENCE OF ANYONE WILL DO THEM ANY GOOD OR HARM. AND KNOW THAT ALLAH ﷻ IS WITH YOU."

UNKNOWN

Justice

I don't know about you, but I sometimes think about the people in this world that do not believe yet still accomplish good deeds. How could these people possibly not see Jannah when they might have done more good that some Muslims in their lifetime?

I then remind myself of three things. First, Allah ﷻ is the Justest and the All Knowing. He does what He pleases according to the best justice, can save and guide even the ones you least expect on His path. If He doesn't, then He knows why.

Second, what is a life spent doing good but forever being ungrateful truly worth? When you know everything He gave us, how merciful He is, how He gives us a higher purpose than this dunya and how He made the signs so clear and accessible... It ends up being hard finding them excuses.

Finally, as much as we disagree and do not fully comprehend these positions, our job is never to try to convince or be disrespectful. Our Creator wants us to represent Islam as best we can, just like the Messenger ﷺ did.

So be kind, wise, just, and leave the rest to Him.

In times like this, people might come up and say "*Ya Allah ﷻ why? Innocent people are dying.*" or "*If God was really fair or even existed, He wouldn't let wars and discriminations happen*".

Now, these people are blaming Allah ﷻ for something only *humans* are responsible for. Yes, He could just stop everything if He wanted to. But He knows best, does not control our emotions and gave us a free will, opportunities for us to spread good and grow closer to Him. He specifically asked us to stand for justice to the best of our ability and trust Him. Indeed, Allah ﷻ is The Utterly Just. In the Afterlife, He will leave no right unestablished. He will punish all those who felt entitled to oppress others. He will punish those who assumed their power justifies doing what only He is supposed to do, aka taking lives.

If someone or you question His fairness, please remember: Allah ﷻ sees and knows all. He holds everyone accountable for everything that they did on Earth. He is the fairest of all, so help as much as you can and trust Him. He did shared this with us: "*Whoever kills an innocent soul [...], it is as if he had slain mankind entirely. And whoever saves one — it is as if he had saved mankind entirely.*" (5:32)

I found it so crazy to see how blinded men are by their egos. How they think they can go against the rules and rule over this world. It's like they're not learning anything from the crisis we've been going during Covid, from the wars they started, from natural disasters… They just keep running after this life instead of looking after a higher purpose or even simply questioning themselves.

This hits me even more when it comes to Muslim countries. It's like an endless race of which one is going to be the richest, which one is going to build the highest building, which one is going to normalise haram practises even more so they can look like Paradise to the disbelievers… All of this while their neighbours, fellow brothers and sisters in Islam, are getting poorer by the day with kids dying of hunger, women being denied education, people being martyred in a genocide and living under occupation. They really, sadly, didn't understand a thing about what being rich as a Muslim means. They have no understand of the word *justice*.

We aren't above anything. When you zoom out, you realise we're literally nothing. I once read something that I thought was brilliant, and that's how I will conclude this part: "*Allah ﷻ owns this world and it is worthless to Him, so it isn't right that we're so attached to it when it doesn't even belong to us*".

"IS NOT ALLAH ﷻ THE MOST JUST OF JUDGES?"

(95:8)

THE PROPHET ﷺ SAID: "HELP YOUR BROTHER WHETHER HE IS AN OPPRESSOR OR AN OPPRESSED," A MAN SAID, "O ALLAH ﷻ'S MESSENGER! I WILL HELP HIM IF HE IS OPPRESSED, BUT IF HE IS AN OPPRESSOR, HOW SHALL I HELP HIM?" THE PROPHET ﷺ SAID, "BY PREVENTING HIM FROM OPPRESSING (OTHERS), FOR THAT IS HOW TO HELP HIM."

AL-BUKHARI, 6952

Knowledge

The more I know, the more I realise how little I *actually* know — is it just me?

I love that the pursuit of knowledge is not only a great reminder of how humble we should be, but also, an incredible source of wealth in all its aspects. Whether it is by going to school, studying the Quran and the Tafsir, learning a new skill, discovering the principles of Fiqh… The possibilities are endless and it is truly one of the best investments you can make for yourself.

It's interesting how we still see people that believe profane sciences are not compatible with being Muslim. And yet, when we look at the history of Islam, we are be able to tell that many scholars and inventors were *in fact* Muslim. If anything, I feel like crossing sciences with Islam simply makes you realise how it is The Truth Subhan'Allah ﷻ. I mean, how many evidences from the Quran align with recent discoveries, whether it be in astronomy, biology or medicine? Increasing our knowledge about different aspects of our lives is an amazing way to see the limits of what human beings can know, and how we were granted with an actual miracle.

You know, when Allah ﷻ said *'Iqra!'* ("*Read!*"), that wasn't just for men.

It's crazy how some people dislike and despise women who cultivate their knowledge. As soon as you encourage learning and investing in yourself, the feminism and westernisation accusations come right at you, as if the first university in the world wasn't founded by a Muslimah (Fatima al-Fihriya, may Allah ﷻ bless her), as if there were never any inspiring, knowledgable and hard-working women in the history of Islam. Nonetheless, culture, generational traumas and society's stigmas are surely to blame, so don't be too hard on those thinking this way yet keep in mind that the right people for you will always encourage you to learn and grow.

So next time someone comes to you and acts like you shouldn't be smart or educated, remember that nowhere in Islam does it say that women can't study, learn and work. If you do it all with the intention to please Allah ﷻ, then you truly have nothing to worry about.

Al-Sha'bi, may Allah ﷻ have mercy on him, said, "The statement 'I do not know' is one half of knowledge."

Al-Darimi, 186

The Prophet ﷺ said, "Knowledge is three types and anything else is a surplus: a decisive verse, or an established Sunnah, or an obligation of justice."

Abi Dawud 2885

Family

I once heard a man say *"The only people on this planet you love unconditionally are your family. You don't choose to part of it like you would with your friends group or your workplace, so you have no other choice but to love them."* I thought this was interesting but probably an unpopular opinion until I had this chat with someone who told me they loved their mom simply because they had to. This was so surprising to me so I asked what they meant and they said "I don't love her because she has specific qualities or a strong bond with her. We share the same blood, she gave birth to me so I love her for that but that's it." I'm not even sure this can be called 'love' but I thought I would respect their opinion.

I'm blessed to love my family not because I *have to* but for everything they have done for me and for all the wonderful memories we have together. This made me realise how I should *never* take them for granted. I completely minimised the amount of people who have toxic families or minimal interactions with them. I find this extremely sad and maybe naively believe that patience, communication and quality time could greatly improve these types of relationships… Unless this is a hardship for you in this dunya.

Please don't feel resentment or contempt towards them, especially your parents. Instead, make du'as and behave like the kid you would like to have. There's a great reward for children who were good to their parents, don't miss out on it.

A man stood for the Prophet ﷺ while he was upon the pulpit, and he said, "O Messenger of Allah ﷻ, who among people are best?" The Prophet said, "The best of people are the most to recite the Quran, the most fearful of Allah ﷻ, the most enjoining of good, the most forbidding of evil, and the most to maintain family relations."

MUSNAD AHMAD 27434

Respect

One of the most important lessons I learned this year is how you should absolutely *never* compromise on the bare minimum. Respect isn't an option, you aren't supposed to ask for it, you should *expect* it.

I made the mistake to let someone walk over me despite knowing my value, or at least I thought so. I was justifying forgiving without setting boundaries for myself, by communicating how I felt, assuming that they would surely realise how wrong their behaviour was at some point, that they had no reason not to do this to me, especially considering the bond we had. Spoiler alert: they never did and never apologised.

It was so nerve wracking for me to witness a person I had been nothing but sincere with disrespecting me in a way that was so blatant. I knew I didn't deserve that, but because of how much I hate giving up on people I care about and how much hope I had for them to purify their heart, I stayed. It was like I thought I would betray myself if I left, until I realised I was actually losing myself so I wouldn't lose them.

Sure, we don't always have the right part and we sometimes hurt people too, but we shouldn't be too proud to ask for forgiveness or minimise the impact of our words and actions. Please respect others' feelings and boundaries like you would like yours to be respected. If not for yourself, then for the sake of Allah ﷻ.

"O ALLAH ﷻ, IF I HAVE INSULTED ANY BELIEVER, THEN PLEASE MAKE IT A REASON FOR HIM TO BE CLOSE TO YOU ON JUDGMENT DAY".

UNKNOWN

"O YOU WHO HAVE BELIEVED, LET NOT A PEOPLE RIDICULE [ANOTHER] PEOPLE; PERHAPS THEY MAY BE BETTER THAN THEM; NOR LET WOMEN RIDICULE [OTHER] WOMEN; PERHAPS THEY MAY BE BETTER THAN THEM. AND DO NOT INSULT ONE ANOTHER AND DO NOT CALL EACH OTHER BY [OFFENSIVE] NICKNAMES. WRETCHED IS THE NAME OF DISOBEDIENCE AFTER [ONE'S] FAITH. AND WHOEVER DOES NOT REPENT - THEN IT IS THOSE WHO ARE THE WRONGDOERS."

(49:11)

Comparison

Sister, life works in cycle, just like our Planet goes through seasons. Don't envy anyone. Don't compare yourself to those who seem to have it all, who seem to have it together. I can guarantee you, no one does.

You know, most of my close friends grew up in pretty wealthy families and that wasn't my case (although I really didn't have to complain Alhamdulillah). I was also never the 'pretty' one in the group which meant that in my early twenties, I would put so much pressure on myself to at least have one thing I didn't have to compare myself with. This turned out to be my studies, until Allah ﷻ decided otherwise.

Failing med school was one of the most notable moments of my life. I was 20 and seeing everyone around being successful at uni made me feel so bad about myself. I remember meeting with my friends and bursting into tears because of how lame I felt being envious of how proud everyone was. Little did I know that choosing another path would turn out to be so beneficial for me. I guess it was my first realisation of people seeing the results but Allah ﷻ seeing the efforts.

Fast forward to now, I still compare myself but in a healthy way that makes me want to improve and work hard rather than making me feel like I need to outperform everyone. I've accepted that we each have our own singularities, life decisions and moments that are specific to us and transform us overtime. There's so much beauty in seeing how one gets up after falling. Like a baby learning how to walk and then run you know?

Being successful, whether it be in your religion or your career, doesn't come at the cost of others achievements. Besides, you were blessed with so much more than you think, with things others might even be comparing themselves to. Indeed, Allah ﷻ is The Sustainer and granted each of us a rizq that can be both a blessing and a trial for us. Yes, money is nice, but what's its worth of it if you don't spend it helping those in need? Same goes with having kids: of course building a family is amazing, but if Allah ﷻ doesn't provide you with that, does that mean you should resent Him? What if He's preserving you from something terrible that drive you away from Him? It is so easy to believe that others have more than you, but make sure to work on yourself. Go back to the story of Prophet Ayyub (as) who had it all until he had nothing left. Be aware of your blessings, know the qualities you have, the ones you want to develop, the flaws you want to get rid off and that this is what the journey of life is all about.

THE PROPHET ﷺ SAID, "NONE OF YOU WILL HAVE FAITH UNTIL HE LOVES FOR HIS BROTHER WHAT HE LOVES FOR HIMSELF."

AL-BUKHARI 13
MUSLIM 45

Intentions

The last couple of months, I've been focusing on myself and trying to reconnect with my faith after dealing with hardships really caught up on me and made me do things mechanically rather than sincerely.

This made me think a lot about intentions. It's crazy how you can so easily fall into a routine of doing acts of worship without aiming to become better, or even worse, do them hoping people will think you're a great Muslim...

But you can also be in a situation where you're too hard on yourself because you're not where you want to be, or you struggle to stop a sin you've been wanting to end for a while. Either way, Sheytan is the best at making you feel superior or worthless, and will always make everything in his power to drive you away from our Creator.

And I know this reminder will feel uncomfortable to some, but I wouldn't honour the name of my page if it wasn't about balance. Of course, Allah ﷻ is The Most Loving, Kind and Merciful, but intentions do not always justify disobeying Him. We simply cannot claim *'yes I sin, but I'm only human and have a good heart, He knows it'* all the time, with no intention of improving as soon as possible. That doesn't mean not being merciful to yourself. Making mistakes and being in denial are simply two different things.

We truly underestimate the power of intentions and how everything you do can be an act of 'Ibadah: praying, taking care of your health and body, working, having meaningful conversations, acquiring knowledge...

The fact these deeds can play in our favor when they will be weighted on the day of judgement all because you did them sincerely with the intention of always pleasing the All Mighty just shows how Merciful it is and how easy Islam actually is Subhan'Allah ﷻ, don't you agree?

So this is my reminder to you: be intentional in everything that you do. Cultivate that desire to please Allah ﷻ in everything that you do. Walk towards Him with humility, with a pure heart, and He'll always come to you running. When everyone will judge your actions and the outcome of your decision, He will reward your resilience through it all and judge what's deep in your heart.

That my friend, is how beautiful our deen is.

THE PROPHET ﷺ

"SUCH A PERSON AS RECITES THE QUR'AN AND MASTERS IT BY HEART, WILL BE WITH THE NOBLE RIGHTEOUS SCRIBES (IN HEAVEN). AND SUCH A PERSON EXERTS HIMSELF TO LEARN THE QUR'AN BY HEART, AND RECITES IT WITH GREAT DIFFICULTY, WILL HAVE A DOUBLE REWARD."

AL-BUKHARI 4937

THE PROPHET ﷺ SAID, "PEOPLE WILL BE GATHERED FOR JUDGMENT BASED ON THEIR INTENTIONS."

SUNAN IBN MAJAH 4230

Mindfulness

Let me tell you a story.

A little over two years ago, when I moved to London and got into my room for the first time, the first thing I got out and put on the shelf over my bed was a Mus'haf. My roommate asked what it was and was so surprised I would do this before emptying my suitcase and adding any other piece of decor. I said 'I can't feel good in a home where there's no Quran.'

People do not realise the power the Quran, the words of Allah ﷻ hold. Do you ever think about all the scientific facts discovered only recently but shared in the Quran over 1445 years ago? Do you ever think about the qualities it teaches you, whether it be kindness, respect, charity or humility? Do you ever reflect upon the way it is perfectly written and organised? Do you ever get blown away by your heart immediately feels at peace as soon as the first words of a surah are recited? Subhan'Allah ﷻ, nothing compares honestly.

Sure it can be complex, and it requires us more than just listening, reading or learning it to fully bond with it. But listen: going step by step is better than not step at all or trying to climb a huge one you're going to fall off from. Be mindful with yourself, and not just when it comes to your relationship with Allah ﷻ and His sacred words, but with all your homes in this life — your planet, your house, your body and of course, your heart.

PROPHET MUHAMMAD ﷺ SAID:
"VERILY, ONE WHO DOES NOT HOLD ANYTHING FROM THE QURAN IN HIS HEART IS LIKE A RUINED HOUSE."

AL TIRMIDHI, 2913

Consciousness

I have a question for you guys: have you ever been in a situation where you'd meet a beggar in the street telling you his story and gave him money without truly knowing if what he said was true? Or helped a friend/a family member who ended up not being there for you when you needed them the most? Or said a warm « *assalamu aleykum* to another hijabi, only for her to ignore you?

If the answer is yes, then maybe you later thought *"if I hadn't helped this person, I would have been able to do this"*, *"people are so ungrateful, they always take advantage of me, I should stop giving"*, *"my ego took a hit, I wish I hadn't done this"*...

Listen, there is no need to hold onto the past. We have this saying in French that goes: *"With 'what ifs' we could put Paris in a bottle"*. Spreading goodness should never be something you regret, especially when it is being done for the sake of Allah ﷻ. You did these things because you know how much He loves them. If people are ungrateful, leave it to Him. He hears and sees. Having *taqwa* is something we should all seek. None of our actions and thoughts go unnoticed to Allah ﷻ, so by making them acts of worship, we're also turning them into sources of reward to compensate all the other times we forget about Him or do things He dislikes.

You know, my life now looks nothing like it used to. I lost some friends after deciding to wear hijab, I stopped going out as much to focus on my deen, my health and my career, I stopped being so angry at the world for being so unjust... And Subhan'Allah ﷻ, I've been feeling much more at peace.

Being conscious of our Creator looking at us at all times and listening not only whenever we talk to Him but also to ourselves is life-changing. Appreciating His signs and and taking action for His sake first invites us to spend our time, the most precious resource we have, wisely, to focus on *now* rather than yesterday and tomorrow, it leads us to find joy in every day we are granted because Allah ﷻ has given us the honour to be Muslim. Alhamdulillah.

I know how it feels to be nostalgic of a time where maybe you didn't have as much discipline or didn't sacrifice as much to please Him. But I once read quote that said "Why would you cry over ruined houses when gorgeous castles are right in front of you?" and that altered my brain chemistry forever. I hope it does the same for you to insha'Allah ﷻ.

And they're in fact so right when they say "now is a gift and that's why it is called the *present*."

THE PROPHET ﷺ SAID, "VERILY, YOU WILL NEVER LEAVE ANYTHING FOR THE SAKE OF ALLAH ﷻ ALMIGHTY BUT THAT ALLAH ﷻ WILL REPLACE IT WITH SOMETHING BETTER FOR YOU."

MUSNAD AHMAD, 23074

"O YOU WHO HAVE BELIEVED, FEAR ALLAH ﷻ AS HE SHOULD BE FEARED AND DO NOT DIE EXCEPT AS MUSLIMS [IN SUBMISSION TO HIM]."

(3:102)

Stewardship

I have always been blown away by nature. Whether I am looking at the sky and its endlessly changing hues, contemplating the immensity of the ocean, serene on the surface until its hidden darkness emerges, or simply thinking about the uniqueness of Earth… I always get overwhelmed by how small I am and how our Creator has truly blessed us with beautiful signs of His existence Subhan'Allah ﷻ.

But these are not the only things Allah ﷻ wanted us to take from nature.

Nature is humble. Nature knows. Nature deeply loves and worships our Creator, fearing to deceive Him to the point it would not even take the responsibility of honouring His Trust at all times. I am talking about the mountain that would crumble to dust as a sign of prostration. I am talking about the ocean that would never be enough to write all His words. I am talking about the space that keeps expanding and that we will never be able to fully explore. Their greatness has not filled them with pride and ignorance, unlike us.

So now is the time to lift the veil of our egos. Let's not only cherish nature as a divine gift, but also admire it as an example of devotion and humility, surrounding us constantly and reminding us of who we should truly be.

"INDEED, WE OFFERED THE TRUST TO THE HEAVENS AND THE EARTH AND THE MOUNTAINS, AND THEY DECLINED TO BEAR IT AND FEARED IT; BUT MAN [UNDERTOOK TO] BEAR IT. INDEED, HE WAS UNJUST AND IGNORANT."

(33:73)

THE PROPHET ﷺ SAID, "THERE IS NONE AMONGST THE MUSLIMS WHO PLANTS A TREE OR SOWS SEEDS, AND THEN A BIRD, OR A PERSON OR AN ANIMAL EATS FROM IT, BUT IS REGARDED AS A CHARITABLE GIFT FOR HIM."

AL-BUKHARI, 2320

Contentment

Don't you think there's something very humbling and comforting finding joy in the simplest things, the simplest moments? Honestly, I cannot tell you how much I love them. In a world where we constantly feel overstimulated, over-solicited, nothing beats being content with the pure simplicity of Allah ﷻ's blessings.

The warmth of the sun on your face, the laughs shared with loved ones, the sight of a mesmerising sunset after a long hike, the smell of coffee in the morning, the crackling sound of a fireplace, the melody of waves crushing on the shore, the serenity found in a quiet moment of reflection by yourself... I feel like these simple joys remind us of the richness of our existence despite this world not being not our final destination, as if Allah ﷻ wanted to give those who are aware of these tiny things a glimpse of the wonders of Jannah.

I've been embracing these for as long as I can remember and have always felt like they made me appreciate Allah ﷻ so much more. In a society that glorifies complexity and excess, Islam encourages us to be content with little, to cherish the essence of what truly matters, to find true fulfillment and happiness in the smallest blessings. We don't need to fill our homes with clothes and gadgets, but we do need to fill our mind with memories and our souls with Allah ﷻ's gifts.

The Prophet ﷺ said, "Verily, Allah ﷻ will put His servant to trial in what He gives him. Whoever is content with what Allah ﷻ has apportioned for him, then Allah ﷻ will bless him in it and expand it. Whoever is not content, he will never be blessed in it."

Musnad Ahmad 20279

Grief

The last past two years have been rough. From learning to accept the absence of my beloved father who I will never get to see again in this dunya to cut off a man who I trusted yet ended up being one the biggest disappointments of my life, I came out of this with a bruised heart and mentally drained. I've had to grieve my dad and my dreams of him seeing my accomplishments, getting married and having kids, but also, all my hopes about building a life with this person.

Although I could have been mad, question the Qadr of Allah ﷻ and gave up on all my efforts to protect my imaan, I actually realised I wouldn't know how to cope without Him Subhan'Allah ﷻ. Did I say things like *'why Dad?? Why us?'* or *'Why did You put this guy on my way if this was going to be the outcome?'*? Of course, because let's be honest — we're only humans and our nature leads us to be blinded by our feelings first (may He forgive us for that).

But once I'd pour my heart out in sujood, that "resentment" would immediately go away. I would ask for *sabr*. I would ask for forgiveness. I would say Alhamdulillah. I would make du'as for them instead of complaining about my situation and realised grief didn't have to be linear. Some days I'll only remember the good times and have a smile on my face, others will feel like a burden. Regardless, Allah ﷻ knows.

A sister once messaged me, asking what she could do to help her friend who had just lost her dad. This is what I wrote:

"*Inna Lillah wa inna Ilayhi Raji'un*, may Allah ﷻ grant your friend with *sabr* and *sakinah* and may we all meet the people we love in Jannah.

I don't know what your friend's experience was but I'll share mine and hope it's helpful insha'Allah ﷻ.

I tried to see the light in all these dark things and told myself it could have been way worse. I saw my dad died and although it was incredibly hard and I prayed for a miracle until the very last second, I still felt grateful for different reasons. The first one is that after so many months suffering physically and mentally, he left this dunya with no pain and looking really peaceful Alhamdulillah. I hated seeing him going through all of this, but cancer does prepare you for death in a way, unlike dying from a heart attack, a car accident or getting killed. This would have been so much harder. It also cleansed him from his sins, meaning Allah ﷻ wanted him to be pure to get back to Him Alhamdulillah.

Finally, having a family that truly understands the beauty and meaning of Islam was what helped the most, because we kept giving each other reminders about death and how as Muslims we are lucky enough to know what's next. We would make lots of du'as, remind ourselves of all the good he did, how my sister and I could now honour his name, and most importantly, about how we will insha'Allah ﷻ meet him again in Jannah.

So that's what you can do: be there for her, share comforting reminders with her and give her time to process and heal...

I'm not going to lie, some days are really hard but I try to remember that if Allah ﷻ took my dad, then that was better for him and for us. I don't think our parents nor Allah ﷻ want us to spend our days crying and not live our lives anymore. Death for Muslims isn't a bad thing, we just need to learn to accept it."

NAFI' REPORTED:

A SON OF ABDULLAH IBN UMAR, MAY ALLAH ﷻ BE PLEASED WITH HIM, COMPLAINED OF AN ILLNESS AND IBN UMAR WAS VERY DISTRAUGHT OVER HIM SO MUCH THAT SOME PEOPLE SAID: WE ARE AFRAID FOR THIS OLD MAN BECAUSE OF WHAT MIGHT HAPPEN TO HIS BOY! THE BOY DIED AND IBN UMAR WENT OUT TO HIS FUNERAL. THERE WAS NOT A MAN MORE VISIBLY HAPPY THAN HIM, SO HE WAS ASKED WHY. IBN UMAR SAID, "VERILY, IT WAS ONLY MERCY FOR HIM AND WHEN THE DECREE OF ALLAH ﷻ CAME TO PASS, WE ACCEPTED IT."

AL-RIDA 'AN ALLAH ﷻ BI-QADA'IHI LI-IBN ABI AL-DUNYA 98

Hope

Over the past few years, I've received my fair share of messages from sisters feeling exhausted and tired of being constantly tested. Honestly, I get you: going through trials and not really 'getting a break' can be mentally draining and lead you to question everything... Unless you *decide* to see the light in the dark. Unless you *decide* to turn these into lessons. Unless you *decide* to take these as a challenge to improve for the sake of Allah ﷻ.

People have become so negative, so pessimistic, but how can we feel that way as Muslims when our religion is all about trusting Allah ﷻ, taking care of our hearts and radiating light? We need to always strive to anchor ourselves in the belief of His wisdom encompassing every aspect of our lives, and while it's natural to experience a range of emotions, our belief in Allah ﷻ's mercy and guidance should serve as a beacon of hope. Besides, your emotions are only defined by your perception of them, so the moment you make it a point to cultivate a positive outlook, to embrace how you feel and realise they are a proof of your humanity, a way for you to go back to Allah ﷻ, then everything changes.

It is through prayer, reflection, and seeking knowledge that we can nurture our imaan, it is by embodying the principles of our deen, by choosing optimism, hope and resilience that we can finally find solace in this dunya. He promised it to us, so believe Him.

"DO NOT LOSE HOPE NOR DESPAIR - IF YOU ARE TRUE BELIEVERS, YOU HAVE THE UPPER HAND."

(3:139)

"DO YOU SUPPOSE THAT YOU WILL ENTER THE GARDEN WITHOUT FIRST HAVING SUFFERED LIKE THOSE BEFORE YOU? THEY WERE AFFLICTED BY MISFORTUNE AND HARDSHIP, AND THEY WERE SO SHAKEN THAT EVEN [THEIR] MESSENGER AND THE BELIEVERS WITH HIM CRIED, 'WHEN WILL GOD'S HELP ARRIVE?' TRULY, GOD'S HELP IS NEAR."

(2:214)

Loneliness

I once read a quote along the ligns of: "*A man was asked how he managed to pray all 5 prayers, and he said « I became certain that no one could stand meeting five times a day, no matter what state I was in — happy, sad, lonely, angry - except the most loving and merciful Allah ﷻ.*"

There is something incredibly peaceful and reassuring about performing Salah but also watching someone pray. The way we lower our heads with humility, how we all do the same specific movements, and quietly talk to our Creator deserves to be embraced more, and especially during the weird times we're currently living.

Salah makes you feel seen and heard on a whole other level. Please don't see it only as an absolute obligation but truly as an opportunity to free your mind from all the dark things inside them. It is like a balm for your heart whenever it's hurt by sadness or loneliness. Take it as a chance to repent, to strengthen your imaan and grow closer to Him. Make it a special moment in your day to look forward to. Pour your soul into it and feel the peace gaining it as He, your Best Friend, listens to you even if He already knows what you'll tell Him.

You might feel lonely, but you're not alone.

I don't know about you guys, but every time I hear converts/reverts telling their stories, it makes me incredibly emotional and reinforces my faith in the most comforting way. Hearing them saying the *shahada* for the first time, being surprised that this simple thing "officially" makes you Muslim, seeing how peaceful their faces look is beautiful... It is wonderful.

It's easy to think that they are the luckiest people, having been able to taste everything that is forbidden in Islam in a past life to then been blessed with the guidance of Allah ﷻ. But it isn't that simple: they often felt lost, like their lives had no purpose or deep meaning. Most of the time, they feel really lonely, having to face families that do not accept their decision, not having Muslim friends, spending Ramadan and Eid alone, and maybe even regretting past things despite the fact they didn't have the knowledge we were given from the start... See, we all have our struggles. You're not alone.

"AND WE HAVE ALREADY CREATED MAN AND KNOW WHAT HIS SOUL WHISPERS TO HIM, AND WE ARE CLOSER TO HIM THAN [HIS] JUGULAR VEIN."

(50:16)

Trust

I'm a problem solver by nature. I thrive from helping people, fixing things, standing against injustice, finding solutions to existing problems by creating stuff... Because of how stubborn I am, I can spend hours, days, even months thinking about how to solve a certain issue. This is probably because I'm the oldest daughter, but also, because I was often the one adults would trust for an important task and that people seek for advice.

And here's the thing: whenever I would solely rely on myself, this aspect of my character would turn out to be pretty draining: my thoughts would get messy, make me feel anxious, even useless, and like there's no light at the end of the tunnel. However, whenever I would decide to do my best and leave the rest to Allah ﷻ, putting all my trust in Him, whatever the result ends up being, the whole journey just feels peaceful, meaningful and right. Subhan'Allah ﷻ.

What you feel is not caused by what you face, but by your mindset. Therefore, the stronger your imaan is, the more it'll shape the way you think and the way you face this dunya, which is through finding comfort in the fact that He knows best, is with the patient, rewards the effort greatly and thus, that everything is gonna be absolutely fine eventually. At the end of the day, the only one you can trust wholeheartedly is Him because He will never betray you or let you down as long as you protect and always strengthen your bond to Him.

So always start with Bismillah, keep going with Astaghfirullah, and finish with Alhamdulillah.

I'll share with you some mindset switches I'm making to calm my heart and deepen my trust in Allah ﷻ:

- *I'm stronger than I think.* Allah ﷻ doesn't burden me with things I cannot bear. There's nothing I can't achieve/overcome as long as I have Sabr and Tawakkul.

- *Gratitude does wonders to the heart.* It fills it with grace and peace. It humbles you. Say Alhamdulillah even for the trials you go through. Being grateful to Allah ﷻ for the simplest things makes loving and living simple.

- *The more I'll trust Allah ﷻ, the more I'll trust myself.* Everything is difficult when I seek it through myself but nothing is when I seek it through the help of Allah ﷻ. I can ask Him anything, He'll always listen. He knows me the best, gives me signs to take the right decisions and blesses me with lessons when I don't see them.

THE PROPHET ﷺ SAID,

"VERILY, YOU WILL NEVER LEAVE ANYTHING FOR THE SAKE OF ALLAH ﷻ ALMIGHTY BUT THAT ALLAH ﷻ WILL REPLACE IT WITH SOMETHING BETTER FOR YOU."

Love

Do you ever wonder if you truly love Allah ﷻ? Sure you worship Him, but what about loving Him? Well, here's some reassurance for you.

Beyond the gratitude you can show to Him which is a beautiful sign of love, you loving people for His sake also highlights how much you love Him. For a long time, I didn't fully comprehend what it meant until I realised there's no better kind of love than this one.

See, loving someone for the sake of Allah ﷻ means they inspire you to grow closer to Islam, they bring out the best in you, that you pray that they're always blessed with His guidance and hope to meet them in Jannah.

But doesn't it also show your love for The Almighty? Doesn't it show that the more you love Him, the more you want to surround yourself with people who remind you of His presence? Through the love for other people, we experience the love between Allah ﷻ and us. So if you've ever doubted or never realised you love Him too, find comfort in the fact that you do in the simplest ways and are on the path to true happiness.

The Prophet ﷺ never missed an opportunity to prove how much Allah ﷻ loves us. In a hadith reported by Bukhari and Muslim, he says:

"When Allah ﷻ loves someone he calls to Jibreel (as) saying: 'O Jibreel, I love such and such a person, so love him.' Then Jibreel will call to the angels of the heavens and say: 'Allah ﷻ loves such and such a person so love him.' And the angels will love [that person]. And then Allah ﷻ will place acceptance on Earth for that believer."

Sometimes I found myself crying when I think about how much He loves me and how I seem to not be sufficiently showing my love back to Him. I tell myself that the journey of offering your whole heart to Allah ﷻ isn't alway easy, but is certainly the key to detach yourself from this worldly life and to find inner peace.

Allah ﷻ highly values love, so be a loving person — with your parents, your partner, your friends, your kids, everyone, including *yourself*.

Let's make it a habit to tell Him how much we love Him and thank Him for the love He gives us even when we forget to do so.

Whenever my imaan is taking a hit, I like to remind myself of the wonderful human being our beloved Prophet ﷺ was. I am sure many of you feel the same way, but thinking of him always brings so much serenity, like a comforting wave of wisdom and kindness wrapping around you, reminding you it's all gonna be okay.

Honestly, I sometimes get surprised by how much I love a man who I have never seen nor met. It just goes beyond being inspired by his character and story, it's about forever being grateful for his legacy, cherishing and honouring it. As soon as I think about this, I ask Allah ﷻ to guide me and bring me closer to his example day by day but also the rest of the Ummah.

You know when you share a reminder with someone and their initial reaction is to say "Yes but I can't be like The Prophet ﷺ"? Well indeed, you can't - however He was chosen as our Messenger for a reason. Allah ﷻ made him our role model for a reason, and in order for us to truly embrace his noble teachings and example, we cultivate our love for him by educating ourselves on his story. We should also strive to embody his character and emulate his actions to the best of our abilities. The more we try, the closer we'll be to Allah ﷻ and the easier it'll be to fulfill our purpose as Muslims.

One of the ideas I used to naively believe in a few years ago is that romantic love was completely different from all the other types of love. I thought it was all about butterflies, attraction, excitement, head rushes, basically things you don't feel with Allah (swt), your family, your friends...

I was wrong. You know why?
Because Love is not an emotion.

This might be *falling* in love, yes.

You get the adrenaline of falling, just as if you were jumping off a cliff. But what happens once you've fallen?

Most people have become blinded by this idea, addicted to these emotions, to the point where they'd rather keep looking to live that rush over and over again, mistaking it for Love, leaving once it's gone, making you just another option, rather than actually discovering what *true* Love is about.

See, you can't solely rely on an emotion to define whether or not you love someone. Emotions, by definition, do *not* last.

Anger is an emotion. Joy is an emotion. Sadness is an emotion. Fear is an emotion.

But Love? Love is so much more than that.

Love is trust. Love is time.
Love is care. Love is presence.
Love is growth. Love is complicity.
Love is effort. Love is a choice.

You choose to swim through the waves and build these stairs to get back up together. You choose to show up, to listen, to confide and remember. You choose to invest time and energy in them. You choose them all day, everyday, all over again. You choose to make du'a for them. You choose them when it's easy, you choose them when it gets rough. You choose them when you're sad, mad, ecstatic, scared, hopeful. You choose them when they're sad, mad, ecstatic, scared, hopeful. You fight for each other. You commit. That's what Love is about.

This Love is inherent to Islam. You being Muslim means you should be loving, never be ashamed to love deeply, but most importantly, sincerely believe that this is Love in its essence, in its truest and purest form. This is the kind of Love that our dear Prophet Muhammad ﷺ and Khadijah (ra) had, the one that makes you feel seen, heard, safe, peaceful, that celebrates you. That's the kind of Love you should pray for.

And if you have it, be grateful for it, cultivate it, show it, cherish it — because trust me, it's probably one of the most precious treasures one can find in the ocean of possibilities that is life.

The Prophet ﷺ said, "If Allah ﷻ loves a person, He calls Gabriel saying, 'Allah ﷻ loves so and-so; O Gabriel! Love him.' Gabriel would love him and make an announcement amongst the inhabitants of the heaven. 'Allah ﷻ loves so-and-so, therefore you should love him also,' and so all the inhabitants of the heaven would love him, and then he is granted the pleasure of the people on the earth."

Al-Bukhari, 3209

"The Winds of Change"

Copyright © [2024] Assia Boukrouh - The Mizaan. All rights reserved. No part of this publication may be reproduced, distributed, or transmitted in any form or by any means, including photocopying, recording, or other electronic or mechanical methods, without the prior written permission of the publisher, except in the case of brief quotations embodied in critical reviews and certain other noncommercial uses permitted by copyright law.

Disclaimer: The views expressed in this publication are those of the author and do not necessarily reflect the official policy or position of any other agency, organisation, employer, or company.

Printed in Great Britain
by Amazon